VIKING
CROWDFUNDING

Viking Crowdfunding Page

Chapter 1:

Types of Crowdfunding

It's a well-known story: you have a great idea, you work out a business plan, form a company and dream about your inevitable success. Then you go to the bank to ask for a small business loan, and... you get denied. Until about a decade ago, this was the end of the road for countless start-ups. In recent years, crowdfunding has become enormously popular as tech-savvy entrepreneurs turn to the online community when traditional funding can't be secured.

Crowdfunding allows smaller and non-traditional businesses to gain a foothold in the market by raising the money they need to launch their organizations. In this book, you're going to learn what crowdfunding is, how it works, and how you can use it to your advantage. We'll look at where you should crowdfund, what your campaign should look like, and how you can bring in investors with this great new method.

Crowdfunding is the method of raising funds through multiple small donations from a range of investors through an online platform. Given that crowdfunding is a relatively recent addition to the world of business, it's easy to track its growth and evolution. Some historians argue that methods such as selling war bonds and artist patronage are pre-cursors to crowdfunding, but crowdfunding as we know it definitely developed in the 1990s. The first large-scale crowdfunding campaign was hosted in 1997 by the English rock band Marillion, who raised $60,000 through online fan donations to fund a U.S. tour. This sparked a trend of artists using crowdfunding to finance their projects and the first crowdfunding platform, ArtistShare, was set up in 2000. From 2008 to 2011, crowdfunding soared in popularity for businesses outside the arts industry, as platforms like IndieGoGo, Kickstarter, and GoFundMe were established.

There are four kinds of crowdfunding, and the type you choose will affect how your campaign runs. Your choice should be based on the type of business you're running, the size of your campaign, and why you're raising the money. Rewards-based and donation-based crowdfunding can be used on all platforms, whereas only certain platforms provide equity or debt crowdfunding- this is why you should decide what method you want to use before choosing a platform.

Rewards-based crowdfunding is when backers receive a reward in return for their donation. There is usually a hierarchy where bigger donations earn larger rewards. This is the most common form of crowdfunding.

Donation-based crowdfunding is when backers do not receive anything in return for their donation, and donate money because they want to help the campaign's cause. This method is usually used by individuals or charities rather than businesses.

Equity crowdfunding is when, instead of rewards, backers receive a small piece of equity in the company. Equity crowdfunding usually aims for larger donations per person than other styles.

Debt crowdfunding is when money is donated to the campaign by "lenders" instead of "donors", who expect to receive their money back, plus interest. Debt crowdfunding is almost exclusively used by individuals rather than businesses, and a lot of the larger crowdfunding platforms don't offer it. If you're interested in debt crowdfunding, check out sites like Lending Club, Prosper, and Funding Circle.

The crowdfunding method you use should complement your business' campaign aims. For example, if you are selling a product, you could have a rewards-based campaign and offer early access to the product as a reward. If you are trying to raise money for business expansion, equity crowdfunding might be more suitable and allow for future investments.

Chapter 2:
Places for Crowdfunding

Crowdfunding is used by entrepreneurs, small and large businesses, charities, and individuals who need financial assistance. There are numerous crowdfunding platforms to choose from, each trying to cater to the specific needs of one or more of these groups. Let's take a look at some of the best crowdfunding platforms, and what each of them can offer you.

Kickstarter. Probably the most famous crowdfunding platform right now, and many people's first choice because its popularity could potentially mean more people see your campaign. They operate on an "all-or-nothing" format, so your backers are refunded if you don't reach your goal. This can be a risk if your company doesn't have much recognition or your campaign isn't marketed well. It's free to create a campaign, but you will be charged a 5% withdrawal fee and 3-5% processing fees. Kickstarter does not offer equity crowdfunding.

IndieGoGo. As well as raising funds via a classic crowdfunding campaign, IndieGoGo has several options to help your business grow. InDemand allows you to continue raising funds and interacting with backers after your campaign has ended. Marketplace allows you to sell the products or services you created with IndieGoGo's help. The China Program helps Western companies to build a bigger audience in China. There is a 5% platform fee for campaigns and InDemand projects. IndieGoGo offers equity crowdfunding.

Crowdfunder. This platform only deals in equity crowdfunding, and charges a flat monthly fee rather than a percentage of your profits. Crowdfunder is best for businesses who have already made a name for themselves and have a network of interested parties. Crowdfunder's users are accredited investors who are looking for new business opportunities. You can choose between their starter plan at $299/month, or their premium plan at $499/month.

RocketHub. The main difference between this platform and others is that RocketHub tries to integrate social media aspects into its site by creating a community of entrepreneurs who will help each other, financially or with business advice. That said, anyone can donate to a RocketHub campaign and like IndieGoGo, you get to keep the funds you raise whether your campaign reaches its goal or not. Between its platform charge and processing fees, RocketHub charges 8% if a campaign reaches its goal and 12% if it doesn't. RocketHub offers equity crowdfunding.

Of course, there are other crowdfunding platforms such as GoFundMe and Kiva out there, but they might focus on other areas like charitable causes and not be suitable for your business. When signing up for any crowdfunding site, your campaign details will be checked to see if it fits the platform, so not doing your research before signing up might cost you a chance to start your campaign immediately.

After you've chosen your crowdfunding method and platform, you can begin to create your campaign. Most platforms will have a step-by-step creation process that shows you how to make the most of that particular site's features. Platforms also usually have downloadable guides that contain information about starting and maintaining your campaign. These are great resources, especially if you haven't used that platform before. Of course, there are some things that you should consider when making your campaign regardless of where you do it. Keep these top tips in mind when setting up your campaign:

Pick your project. Are you raising funds to launch a product or service, grow your business, or something else? You need to have a clearly-defined plan for the money you raise, otherwise backers will not donate. It's also important that you can show backers what you're doing with their money once your campaign is funded. This is much easier to do with a project that has tangible results, like a new product or premises.

Plan a multimedia pitch. When it comes to drawing in potential backers, you have a lot of weapons in your arsenal, such as images, video, audio, and text. Your first step should be to have an eye-catching thumbnail and title that will be shown on the platform and on any social media where you share the campaign- these elements need to draw people in. Once someone has clicked on your page, use video to show what your company is doing, and have a strong written pitch to convince them you're worth backing.

Tell a story. Your new backers will either know very little or absolutely nothing about the story behind your company. The best way to get someone to connect with your campaign is to tell them who you are, what you're doing, and why you're doing it. Show them how you've reached the point you're at right now, why you care about the project you're trying to fund, and what your hopes for the company's future are.

Chapter 2:

Maximizing Crowdfunding

You've chosen your platform and your campaign has been set up- now the real fun begins! The key to running a successful crowdfunding campaign is regular communication with your backers and potential backers. Your communication needs to be clear, interesting to read/watch, and easy to find. Let's go through a few steps that will help you run the ultimate crowdfunding campaign.

Choose your campaign length. When you create a campaign, you'll have to choose how long it should be- you can usually change this length later, but it's best to decide at the very beginning. Campaigns can be anywhere from one day to sixty or ninety, depending on the site you use. Each platform has its own recommendation when it comes to how long your campaign should be, but the average is between thirty and forty days. This kind of length shows that you're confident that you can raise the money, and gives enough time to raise awareness without losing people's interest.

Share on social media. It's imperative that you don't rely on the platform you're using to market your campaign for you. A lot of your backing will come from people you know personally, particularly if you're a smaller business. Reach out to friends, family, professional peers and potential investors through every social media channel you can. Make the campaign clearly visible on your website or Facebook page, and share it on as many sites as possible in order to reach a broad spectrum of potential backers. It's also a good idea to share any photos or videos you have on your campaign in order to pique people's interest as they scroll through their feeds.

Learn from the best. There's a lot you can learn from guides and rulebooks, but sometimes the best way to learn about success is to follow a good example. Go to your crowdfunding platform and check out some of their most successful campaigns. What grabs your attention? Would you back this campaign, and why? What are they doing that you aren't? Asking yourself these questions will help you to create a campaign people want to support.

Give regular updates. Don't forget about your backers once they've donated! Crowdfunding backers are donating money to your project because they have a strong interest, and they'll want to see how things are going. Project updates will also attract new backers, especially if you make sure to share your updates on social media. People are more likely to donate to something when they can see evidence of it coming together.

Have interesting rewards. Obviously, this step only applies if you've chosen to use a rewards-based method, but having multiple reward levels can create a great incentive for backers to donate larger amounts. How many rewards levels you have is up to you, but it can be useful to offer rewards for specific amounts in order to encourage slightly larger donations. Many campaigns have a series of small reward items that they build up as a backer donates more money. For example, if you were creating a film, you might have three levels: $10, $20, and $50. The $10 level would be the lowest level that earns a reward, and this would usually be some form of acknowledgement, like a film credit. At $20, you would reward a backer with a film credit and something else, like a film script. At $50, you would then offer both of the lower rewards and another reward, such as an invitation to the premiere of the film. These incentives can cause backers to donate more money than they'd otherwise planned, so make sure your rewards are exciting!

Conclusion

Crowdfunding is a fast-growing industry and this is a great time to get involved. Whether you're a small business who wants to be bigger or you have a great invention that the world needs to see, crowdfunding will give you the financial opportunities that used to only be available to big institutions. Choose the project you want to fund, decide which crowdfunding method and platform suits it best, and get to work! Use every tool in your arsenal (and in this book) to create an eye-catching campaign, then market it thoroughly for as long as you deem necessary. By the end of this process, you'll have a well-funded campaign and a base for future success.

www.ingramcontent.com/pod-product-compliance
Lightning Source LLC
Chambersburg PA
CBRC090852210326
41597CB00011B/175